Design   David West · Children's Book Design
Illustrations   George Thompson
Picture Research Cee Weston-Baker

The publishers wish to thank
Nigel Norris B.V.Sc. M.R.C.V.S.
for his assistance in the
preparation of this book.

Published in Great Britain in 1988 by
Franklin Watts, 12a Golden Square, London W1

© Aladdin Books Ltd

Designed and produced by
Aladdin Books Ltd, 70 Old Compton Street, London W1

ISBN 0 86313 800 4

Printed in Belgium

Contents

FIRST PETS

Guinea Pigs

Kate Petty

Franklin Watts
London · New York · Toronto · Sydney

The guinea pig

Guinea pigs are sometimes called cavies. Wild cavies were first found in South America. They belong to the same big family of animals as hamsters and squirrels. Guinea pigs have been kept as pets for about 400 years. They make very good pets for children because they are gentle and easy to tame. They usually live for about five years.

Pretty guinea pigs like this smooth-haired one can be bought from most pet shops.

Wild cavies probably looked like this Golden Agouti guinea pig

All sorts of guinea pigs

What sort of guinea pig would you choose? One with smooth hair or one with rough hair growing in little rosettes? Some guinea pigs have very long, silky hair which covers their faces so that you can't tell which end is which! There are many different coloured guinea pigs. Some of the light-coloured ones have pink eyes.

Three different sorts of coats

smooth-haired guinea pig

Peruvian guinea pig

Abyssinian (rosette) guinea pig

A Tortoiseshell Peruvian is usually only available from a breeder

Looking at a guinea pig

Guinea pigs are prettier than many of their rodent cousins. As with all rodents, their teeth are made for gnawing. The front teeth, called incisors, never stop growing. Guinea pigs need hard food to wear them down. A full-grown guinea pig is 20-25 cms long. It has short ears, short legs and no tail. Healthy guinea pigs have bright eyes and glossy hair.

The guinea pig has long front teeth for gnawing.

All guinea pigs have the same smooth, rounded shape, like this Grey Agout

On the move

Guinea pigs scuttle about quickly on their short legs but they cannot jump or climb. Guinea pigs need as much space as possible to run about in. If they don't have enough exercise they can become fat. Guinea pigs in a run need to be protected from other animals. The run should be covered on all sides, including underneath, with wire netting.

A run like this can be moved every few days to provide fresh grass for the guinea pigs.

Guinea pigs have four toes on their front feet but only three on their back feet

Eating

Wild cavies spend their lives grazing on the grasslands. Pet guinea pigs spend a lot of time eating, too. They need to be fed twice a day. They must have a mixture of dry grains and fresh food. Root vegetables, like carrots, and leaves, such as lettuce and dandelion, keep a guinea pig healthy. It also needs plenty of water to drink.

Water stays fresher in a bottle than in a bowl.

A carrot helps to wear down the incisors as well as providing vitamins.

Sociable guinea pigs

Guinea pigs in the wild live in large groups. One living alone in captivity can get lonely. Several female guinea pigs will live together happily but two boars in the same cage will almost certainly fight. A guinea pig will willingly share its cage with a rabbit, but if it has to live alone it will need lots of attention from its owner to keep it happy.

Guinea pigs are naturally timid creatures.

Guinea pig friends will often huddle togethe

Chatterboxes

Guinea pigs are friendly little creatures once they are used to people, and become very tame. They soon learn when it is feeding time and will run around giving loud squeaks of excitement. Guinea pigs are very chatty. They have a whole range of sounds, from noisy squeaks to a variety of contented little grunts and chirrups.

Guinea pigs will often take food from your hand.

This guinea pig is looking to see if its next meal is on the way.

Newborn guinea pigs

Most rodents are pregnant for 21 days and their babies are born blind, hairless and helpless. Guinea pigs are pregnant for 68 days. Newborn guinea pigs have open eyes, hair and even all their teeth. The mother usually has two or four babies – and occasionally six. She can only feed two at a time.

The babies feed from their mother for the first three weeks of their lives.

This guinea pig is only a few minutes old but soon it will be on its feet.

Growing up

A newborn guinea pig can run around only an hour after it is born. It weighs 85-90 g. By the time it is fully grown – at about six months – it will be ten times that weight. When they are eight weeks old, pet guinea pigs can go to new homes – and they can even start having babies of their own.

8-10 weeks – 12-15 cms

newborn – 7cms

1 year – 20-25 cms

Abyssinian mother and babies

Handle with care

Guinea pigs hardly ever bite or scratch. Be very careful not to drop a guinea pig because it can be badly hurt by a fall. Hold it firmly when you pick it up. Support the weight of its hindquarters with one hand and grasp it around the shoulders with the other. It will respond to being stroked with little chattering noises.

The correct way to pick up a guinea pig.

An Abyssinian's rosettes can be carefully groomed with a toothbrush

Know your guinea pigs

This chart will help you to recognise some
of the different breeds of guinea pigs.
A special guinea pig show is the best place
to see them. Guinea pigs vary in hair type
and colour. Breeders are always trying to
find new variations. A full-grown guinea pig
is about the same size as a man's shoe.

Roan Abyssinia

Short-haired Self Black

Tricolour Sheltie

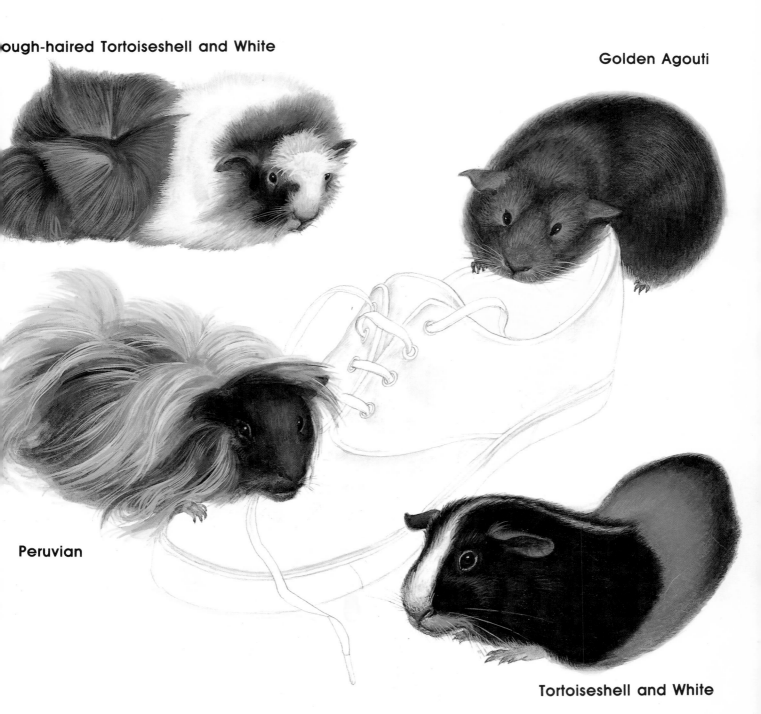

Rough-haired Tortoiseshell and White

Golden Agouti

Peruvian

Tortoiseshell and White

23

Index

Photographic credits:

Cover and pages 19 and 21: Zefa; pages 3, 5, 7, 9, 11, 13 and 17: Bruce Coleman; page 15: Sally Anne Thompson/ Animal Photography.

PRINTED IN BELGIUM BY

proost
INTERNATIONAL BOOK PRODUCTION